Ayudantes de la comunidad / Helping the Community

¿Qué hacen LOS DOCTORES?
What Do DOCTORS Do?

Amy B. Rogers
Traducido por Eida de la Vega

PowerKiDS press.

New York

Published in 2016 by The Rosen Publishing Group, Inc.
29 East 21st Street, New York, NY 10010

First Edition

Editor: Katie Kawa
Book Design: Katelyn Heinle
Spanish Translator: Eida de la Vega

Photo Credits: Cover (doctor), p. 1 william casey/Shutterstock.com; cover (hands) bymandesigns/Shutterstock.com; series back cover Zffoto/Shutterstock.com; p. 5 Jovan Mandic/Shutterstock.com; p. 6 Ilike/Shutterstock.com; p. 9 Levent Konuk/Shutterstock.com; pp. 10, 24 (coat) michaeljung/Shutterstock.com; pp. 13, 24 (nurse) Konstantin Chagin/Shutterstock.com; p. 14 LWA/The Image Bank/Getty Images; p. 17 Odua Images/Shutterstock.com; p. 18 wavebreakmedia/Shutterstock.com; pp. 21, 24 (medicine) Miodrag Gajic/E+/Getty Images; p. 22 racorn/Shutterstock.com.

Library of Congress Cataloging-in-Publication Data

Rogers, Amy B.
 What do doctors do? = ¿Qué hacen los doctores? / Amy B. Rogers.
    pages cm. — (Helping the community = Ayudantes de la comunidad)
Parallel title: Ayudantes de la comunidad.
In English and Spanish.
 Includes bibliographical references and index.
ISBN 978-1-4994-0620-7 (library binding)
1. Physicians—Juvenile literature. 2. Medical care—Juvenile literature. I. Title.
R690.R589 2015
610—dc23

Manufactured in the United States of America

CPSIA Compliance Information: Batch #WS15PK: For Further Information contact Rosen Publishing, New York, New York at 1-800-237-9932

CONTENIDO

CONTENTS

Los doctores te ayudan cuando estás enfermo.

Doctors help you when you are sick.

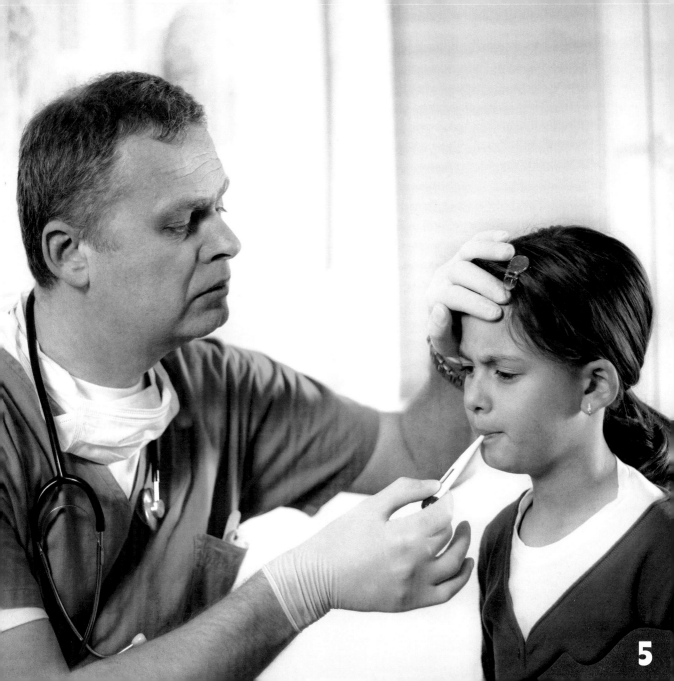

También te ayudan
a mantenerte saludable.

They also help you stay healthy.

¡Algunos doctores solo atienden a niños!

Some doctors are just for kids!

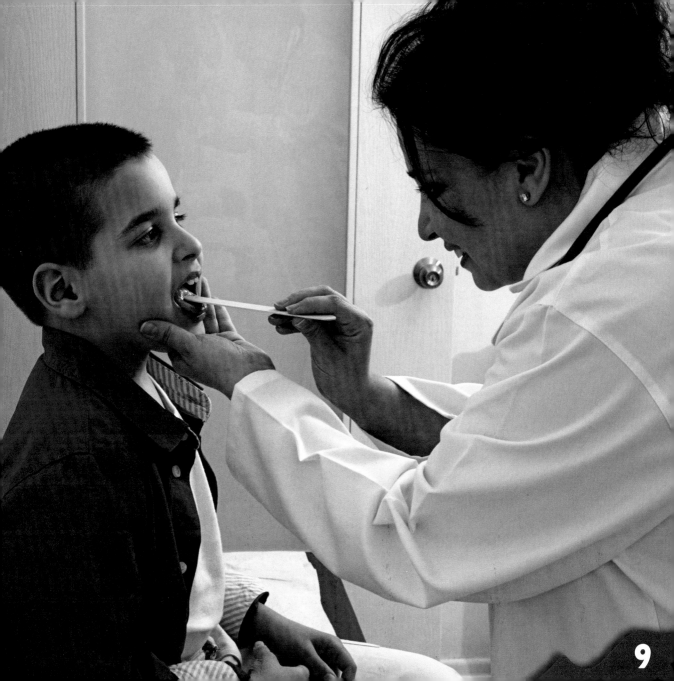

Muchos doctores usan **batas** blancas.

Many doctors wear white **coats**.

Los doctores tienen ayudantes.
Son **enfermeras** o **enfermeros**.

Doctors have helpers.
They are called **nurses**.

El doctor te mide para saber
tu altura.

A doctor sees how tall you are.

El doctor escucha tu corazón.

A doctor listens to your heart.

El doctor te mira los oídos,
la nariz y la garganta.

A doctor looks at your ears,
nose, and throat.

Si estás enfermo, el doctor puede darte **medicina**. La gente toma medicina para sentirse mejor.

If you are sick, a doctor can give you **medicine**. People take medicine to feel better.

¿Te gustaría ser doctor cuando seas mayor?

Would you like to be a doctor when you grow up?

PALABRAS QUE DEBES APRENDER
WORDS TO KNOW

(la) bata
coat

(la) medicina
medicine

(la) enfermera/
(el) enfermero/nurse

ÍNDICE / INDEX

SITIOS DE INTERNET / WEBSITES

Due to the changing nature of Internet links, PowerKids Press has developed an online list of websites related to the subject of this book. This site is updated regularly. Please use this link to access the list: www.powerkidslinks.com/htc/doc